The Missing Snows of KILIMANJARO

T0332570

Rob Waring, *Series Editor*

NATIONAL GEOGRAPHIC
LEARNING

Australia · Brazil · Canada · Mexico · Singapore · United Kingdom · United States

Words to Know

This story is set in Africa, in the country of Tanzania [tænzəniə]. It happens on a mountain called Mount Kilimanjaro [kɪləməndʒɑroʊ].

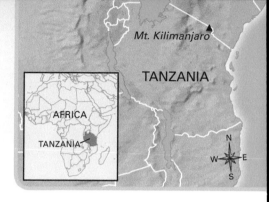

A **The Snows of Kilimanjaro.** Read the paragraph. Then match each word or phrase with the correct definition.

Mount Kilimanjaro is in a hot, tropical region of Africa. It's only a short distance from the equator. It's the highest mountain in Africa and, even though the nearby areas are hot, the mountain's top is covered with glaciers and large ice fields. The peak is very high so it is cool enough to have ice and snow. Recently, however, there has been less ice and snow on Kilimanjaro. Many people think that this is happening due to climate change.

1. tropical region _____

2. equator _____

3. glacier _____

4. peak _____

5. climate change _____

a. a large mass of ice which slowly moves

b. the highest point on a mountain

c. a hot and sometimes wet area of the world

d. the variation in the earth's global weather over time

e. an imaginary line around the exact middle of the earth

glaciers

peak

Mount Kilimanjaro

B **Climate Change.** Read the definitions. Then complete the paragraph with the correct form of the words or phrases.

global warming: an increase in world temperatures caused by gases that stop heat from escaping into space
ice cap: a large mass of ice that covers a particular area
melt: turn from something solid into something soft or liquid
satellite: a piece of equipment that travels through space receiving and sending signals or collecting information
source: the place where something comes from

There are many causes of climate change. One of these causes, known as (1)_____, may be directly affecting Mount Kilimanjaro. As the earth has gotten warmer, the ice and snow on Kilimanjaro have (2)_____. Photographs from a (3)_____ in space show how bad the problem is. Much of the (4)_____ at the top of the mountain has disappeared in the last few years. This is a big problem, because the mountain's snow and iceare an important water (5)_____ for the people in the area.

a satellite

3

ount Kilimanjaro is so high that it is often called the **roof**[1] of Africa. The mountain rises 19,340 **feet**[2], or nearly four **miles**[3], into the sky. It is the highest point on the entire African continent.

Mount Kilimanjaro is in northeastern Tanzania, which is in East Africa. It lies almost exactly between the two cities of Cairo, Egypt, to the north and Cape Town, South Africa, to the south. It is around 220 miles south of the equator and in a hot, tropical region of the world.

---

[1]**roof:** the covering that forms the top of a building; top
[2]**feet:** 1 foot = 0.31 meters
[3]**miles:** 1 mile = 1.61 kilometers

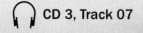 CD 3, Track 07

The impressive snow-covered peaks of Kilimanjaro have been an **inspiration**[4] to visitors for a very long time. Over the years, thousands of people have traveled to Tanzania to climb this **majestic**[5] mountain. Many others have come to view its famous glacier-covered peak.

One of these visitors was a famous American writer named Ernest Hemingway. He wrote a story about the mountain that made it famous. The story, first published in 1936, is called 'The Snows of Kilimanjaro'. In the story, Hemingway describes the mountain's ice fields as "wide as all the world," "great," "high," and "unbelievably white in the sun."

---

[4]**inspiration:** someone or something that makes a person work hard or be creative
[5]**majestic:** very beautiful or powerful in a way that people respect

Ernest Hemingway

As Hemingway wrote, the ice fields on Mount Kilimanjaro are certainly impressive. Although the ice cap is fantastic to see, it does in fact have a much more important purpose. The glaciers on the mountain were formed more than 11,000 years ago. They have become a very important source of water for drinking and farming for people who live in the areas around Kilimanjaro.

Unfortunately, for the last hundred years the snows of Kilimanjaro have been disappearing. This has put this essential water source and beautiful sight at risk. Some of the beautiful snows of Kilimanjaro are now missing. But just how much snow is gone?

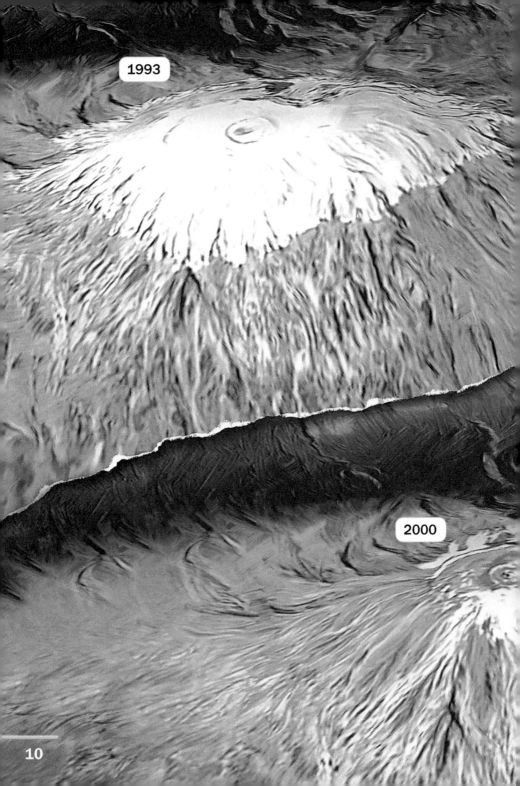

1993

2000

Since 1912, Kilimanjaro's glaciers have gotten more than 80 percent smaller. The significant changes that are happening on the mountain are becoming more and more apparent. A **NASA**[6] satellite has been taking pictures of the mountain's ice cap for more than 15 years. The pictures that the satellite took of Kilimanjaro in 1993 are extremely different from those that were taken only seven years later, in the year 2000. They indicate that there have been very big changes on the mountain. There has been a great reduction in the amount of ice in Kilimanjaro's ice cap.

---

[6]**NASA (National Aeronautics and Space Administration):** a U.S. organization that is responsible for space travel and the scientific study of space

The Effects of Climate Change on Kilimanjaro

There are many different ideas about why Kilimanjaro's snow is disappearing so quickly. For one thing, the mountain is in a tropical region, so the glaciers are particularly at risk for the negative effects of climate change. One type of climate change that may be directly affecting Kilimanjaro is called global warming. This worldwide problem is causing a **gradual**[7] increase in the earth's temperature. As the world's temperatures rise, the snows melt.

---

[7]**gradual:** slow and continuous

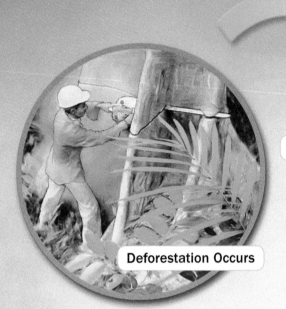

Deforestation Occurs

Air Temperature Rises

How Deforestation Affects Kilimanjaro

Atmosphere Becomes Dryer

Snow Melts

Deforestation[8] is another possible reason that Kilimanjaro glaciers are melting. When trees are cut down in large numbers, the effects can cause changes in the **atmosphere**[9] and the climate. Trees keep the air cooler and help maintain the water levels in the atmosphere. This helps to create clouds and **precipitation**[10] in the form of rain or snow. If there are fewer trees, then this process is affected. The reduced levels of precipitation and increased temperatures can hurt the glaciers.

---

[8]**deforestation:** the cutting down of trees in a large area
[9]**atmosphere:** the gases around the earth
[10]**precipitation:** water that comes from clouds such as rain or snow

Whatever the causes may be, the snows of Kilimanjaro are continuing to melt at a very fast rate. Experts now predict that the mountain's glaciers could completely disappear by the year 2020.

The loss of Kilimanjaro's glaciers would likely cause many problems for the area around the mountain as well as for the earth. It would remove an important source of water for the people who live on or near the mountain. It could also reduce the number of tourists who come to Tanzania to see the beautiful peak. This would also reduce the amount of money that tourists bring to the country. These changes could eventually have serious effects on Tanzania.

Identify Cause and Effect

Circle the cause and underline the effect in each of the sentences.

1. Because Mount Kilimanjaro is in a tropical region, its glaciers are particularly at risk with global warming.

2. Deforestation often results in changes to the atmosphere.

3. Kilimanjaro's glaciers may disappear by 2020 because the ice caps are melting so fast.

In the end, the missing snows of Mount Kilimanjaro may be a warning. They definitely show people all over the world the dangers of climate change and deforestation. They also show how quickly nature can react and change as a result of these dangers.

Hopefully people will learn from the loss of Kilimanjaro's ice cap. Earth's natural riches may not always be around. If these environmental problems are not corrected, we may lose them. Sadly, the majestic snows of Kilimanjaro that so impressed Hemingway may not be available for the world to enjoy forever.

After You Read

1. Kilimanjaro is called the roof of Africa because:
   A. It covers the whole continent.
   B. It's the biggest mountain in Kenya.
   C. It is very high.
   D. Its top is in a tropical region.

2. Ernest Hemingway's description of Kilimanjaro shows that he:
   A. was amazed by it
   B. was scared of it
   C. hated it
   D. was shocked by it

3. In paragraph 1 on page 8, 'they' refers to the:
   A. farmers
   B. glaciers
   C. animals
   D. mountains

4. What important resource do local people get from the mountain?
   A. ice
   B. earth
   C. snow
   D. water

5. What is the purpose of page 11?
   A. to explain how a satellite works
   B. to talk about NASA's environmental efforts
   C. to tell about the recent changes on Kilimanjaro
   D. to introduce a new technology

6. Why is Mount Kilimanjaro especially at risk from environmental change?
   A. The heat of the area melts the snow easily.
   B. The tropical weather helps trees grow.
   C. The tropical weather decreases the earth's temperature.
   D. The cold at the top creates more ice.

7. Which is a suitable heading for page 12?
   A. Global Warming May Be Cause of Missing Snow
   B. Ice and Snow Completely Disappear
   C. Occasional Climate Change Melts Snow
   D. Glacier Remains Unchanged

8. Why are trees important on Kilimanjaro?
   A. They help to create precipitation.
   B. They cause deforestation.
   C. They stop the ice.
   D. They help dry the air.

9. In paragraph 1 on page 16, 'rate' can be replaced by:
   A. distance
   B. speed
   C. time
   D. height

10. In 2025, Tanzania might have _____ water and
   _____ tourists.
   A. less, more
   B. more, less
   C. less, fewer
   D. fewer, no

11. People should take the changes happening on Kilimanjaro
   _____ a warning.
   A. by
   B. as
   C. if
   D. of

12. What is this purpose of this story?
   A. to educate people about how the planet is changing
   B. to talk about Ernest Hemingway's writing
   C. to show how people can help the environment
   D. to tell the history of an African mountain

http://www.save*the*earth.com

The Melting of the Arctic Ice Cap

Scientists have been measuring the gradual disappearance of glacial ice and ice caps on mountain peaks for many years. Most of them have concluded that global warming is part of the problem. The results of this type of climate change are easy to see in places like Mount Kilimanjaro. There, satellite photos have clearly shown how much snow and ice have disappeared in the last few years. However, the problem is much bigger than that. Scientists are particularly concerned about what is happening in the Arctic region. They are especially worried about what is happening to the huge ice cap that covers the top of the earth: the Arctic ice cap.

Side by Side Comparison of Changes in Arctic Sea Ice

1979   2003

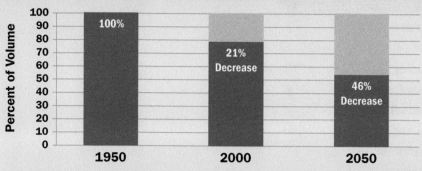

Decrease in the Volume of the Arctic Ice Cap

Percent of Volume

100%

21% Decrease

46% Decrease

1950　　　　2000　　　　2050

This chart shows the percentage of decrease in the size of the Arctic ice cap from the 1950s to now, and the percentage of decrease that scientists predict by 2050.

Temperatures in the Arctic region are rising rapidly—about twice as fast as in other parts of the world. As a result, the ice cap in the Arctic is getting smaller and thinner. Scientists estimate that every year, the Arctic region is losing 9 percent of its ice. At that rate, by the end of the century there may be no more ice left. The Arctic has been covered with ice for at least 50 million years. The effects of a change this large are certain to be felt all over the world.

The Arctic ice melt has already had serious effects on the plants, animals, and native people in the Arctic region. There is much less water for drinking and growing plants. Polar bears and whales have changed their habits. This is making it harder for local hunters to meet their food and clothing needs. The rising level of the sea has forced entire native villages along the coast to move further inland. As the melt continues, countries thousands of miles further south will also be affected. Some scientists predict that sea levels in the United States could rise by as much as three feet by the year 2100. This is something for all of us to think about!

CD 3, Track 08

Word Count: 350
Time: _____

Vocabulary List

atmosphere (14, 15, 17)
climate change (2, 3, 12, 14, 19)
deforestation (14, 15, 17)
equator (2, 4)
feet (4)
glacier (2, 5, 7, 8, 11, 12, 15, 16, 17)
global warming (3, 12)
gradual (12)
ice cap (3, 8, 11, 17, 19)
inspiration (7)
majestic (7, 19)
melt (3, 12, 14, 15, 16, 17)
mile (4)
peak (2, 7, 16)
precipitation (15)
roof (4)
satellite (3, 5, 11)
source (3, 8, 16)
tropical region (2, 4, 12, 17)